THE
SIMPLE ART
OF
FUNDRAISING

Easy Principles and Practices
To Raise the Money You Need

DAMIAN SINCLAIR

Library of Congress Cataloging-in-Publication Data available.

ISBN: 978-1-53052-595-9
Printed in the United States of America

Book design:
Peter Gloege / LOOK Design Studio

Editorial development and creative design support by Ascent:
www.itsyourlifebethere.com

Follow Damian:
 AccelARTllc @AccelARTllc www.AccelARTllc.com

This book is dedicated to
Sara Sinclair,
a woman who supported so many
of my leaps of faith.

CONTENTS

1 :: Leap of Faith 9

2 :: The Donor 13

3 :: Making the Case 23

4 :: The Ask 31

5 :: Thank You 43

6 :: Cultivation 55

7 :: Fundraising Data and Tools 63

8 :: Institutional Giving 77

9 :: Recruiting Others 87

10 :: Conclusion 97

1

LEAP OF FAITH

FEAR. That's what grips many people when they first think about fundraising. Often it is fear about seeking out and meeting potential donors, or even writing letters or emails to ask for funds. These fears are often based on the unknown. What if they say no? I don't know how to ask for money. Maybe I'll offend someone.

Sometimes to conquer your fears you have to take a leap of faith. I know.

Starting my company has been one of my biggest leaps of faith. I watched my wife die after a long battle with an untreatable and incurable disease. This threw me into a tailspin of depression, uncertainty, and fear. I struggled to work and care for my young son. Eventually I quit my job and dedicated time to try to find myself. I needed space, I needed time, and most of all I needed to determine what my next step would be.

During that time of reflection I thought back on what truly made me happy. It was the artists I had served over the years—the passionate and driven visionaries creating some of the country's most exciting work. I was always inspired not only by their artistic creations, but also the bravery they showed in their own lives. I took a leap of faith and founded a company to support these amazing people. I decided to take a huge risk during a time of incredible darkness in the hope that it would someday pay off and I would find myself creating the work the world and I needed.

I continue to derive inspiration from the bravery of the artists I work with and from people like you who continue to take artistic leaps of faith every day.

I learned quickly, though, that the bravery shown in choosing to be an artist did not necessarily translate into bravery—or know-how—when it came to fundraising. I found I needed to help my clients past the perceived giant chasm that is the struggle for enough money to support their work. I needed to dispel some of the myths and fears so they could take a different leap of faith and ask people to support their work.

This book contains the simple and effective principles and practices I teach my clients, and I'm offering them here so that you can also overcome your fundraising fears with know-how and confidently take your next leap of faith. I write from the perspective of the performing arts because so much of my experience comes from that world; however, these principles are universal and can be used in any fundraising situation.

I have raised a lot of money in my career. I helped run a $125 million capital campaign for a major regional theater. I secured funding to create and launch a major performance festival in Washington, DC. I raised more than $200,000 in pledges to allow a 40-year-old arts center build a cash reserve and prepare for its next 40 years. I have made the six-figure ask and have celebrated the $10 donation. Now I help my clients and visionaries like you raise the money they need to achieve their artistic goals.

My personal story is one of fear and risk, which I would argue is not very different from yours. You take bold risks every day you decide to create art for the world. Through my journey I have found many people who were there and wanted to support me. I believe there are a multitude of people in your world who want to support you. This book is offered to help you find those people and get them to support, whether it's to fund the creation of a new artistic work or keep the lights on in your arts center. More specifically, this book is about how to build strong connections with your supporters. I will focus a lot on the individual donor because they are the most abundant category of supporter. These principles are, however, universal and will resonate successfully with institutional and other supporters. I add some information specific to these types of funders toward the end of the book.

From my years in the field of fundraising and helping artists, I want to dispel some myths: Fundraising is portrayed as scary, difficult, and something no one ever wants to do. This causes many to back away and stay focused on the part of the artistic endeavor they love: the creation, the thing that is their passion. Unfortunately, many remain struggling, their bigger goals unfulfilled because of lack of funds. What I will teach you in this book is that all the scary stories and warnings are just myths. Fundraising is simple.

Once you have the right tools and understanding, you will find that the hardest part of fundraising—and the hardest part of any leap of faith—is simply taking the first step.

Let me help you begin.

2

THE DONOR

A WELL-ESTABLISHED dancer decided it was finally time to ask a longtime supporter for a large gift. She set up a lunch meeting to do an "Ask." When the donor responded that he did not have enough to give, the dancer swore off making large Asks, and did not do another one until I started working with her.

Two very similar small arts organizations in the same city did what so many groups do: rushed to get their one solicitation of the year out right before the end of December, believing that donors need to get those last-minute tax breaks in. Both solicitations arrived in my mailbox on the same day.

I have witnessed large fundraising teams at big organizations insulate themselves from the actual donors. Lots of work is getting done, but very few people are going out to meet with or talk to their donors by phone. Too many fundraising positions are filled by people who are afraid to have an actual conversation with their supporters.

The issue in each of these scenarios is the same.

WHO *ARE* YOUR DONORS? DO YOU REALLY KNOW?

So many of the barriers we face in fundraising come from our own misunderstandings about the people who support us—our donors—and why they contribute to us and our creative pursuits. In this chapter I will tackle some of the myths we collectively hold about donors, paint a picture of who your donors really are, and share ideas about ways you can connect with them.

We need to start here, because it's critical to debunk some of the myths we believe about supporters. That's because they act as stumbling points in our quest to raise support for our efforts. For many of us, the mental picture of who is *a* donor, let alone *our* donor, creates our first challenge to overcome in fundraising. If from the beginning you don't know what a donor looks like, how are you going to find one?

Here, then, are some of the common myths about donors.

MYTH #1: YOU DON'T KNOW WHO YOUR DONORS ARE.

Many times clients and organizations have told me that they don't know who to ask for donations. I promise: Your donors are out there. *Right there in front of you, in fact.* They are following you and rooting for you to succeed. Hard to believe, but they are there just waiting to be asked to help.

You can find your donors among:

- » Your volunteers
- » People who sign up on your mailing list
- » Friends and family

» Ticket buyers

» Social media followers

The fact is, you touch more people than you think on a daily basis. The key is tuning in to your ever-growing list of connections and thinking about them as potential supporters.

Fact: Your donors are all around you already.

MYTH #2: ALL THE DONOR CARES ABOUT IS A TAX DEDUCTION.

It's crucial to take down this myth right up front. Deep down you probably don't believe that *all* a donor cares about is a tax deduction. We sure do spend a lot of time, however, expressing that belief to our communities. Why else would we all send end-of-year solicitations? Why else remind people over and over that they can receive a tax deduction for their gift? Why do we worry so much about sending out the tax deduction letter when a gift comes in, instead of just saying "thank you"? Understand that saving money on their taxes is actually a very minor factor in most donors' decision making.

Here's what your donors care about:

» Your mission or vision

» Your work itself

» How donating makes them feel as a
co-contributor to your vision or work

15

» The sense of being a part of something greater than or beyond themselves

» You

Fact: Your donor wants to play a part in your work. It helps them to feel fulfilled.

MYTH #3: THERE IS ONE MAJOR DONOR OUT THERE WHO WILL COVER ALL YOUR NEEDS WITH ONE BIG CHECK.

Wouldn't it be great if that super-rich person in our community just wrote us a big check? Of course it would! That's the fantasy.

While there are major donors in the world, many of them have found their causes and are already actively supporting them. That's not to say you won't someday find your own major donor, but don't put all your hopes in that basket. Your major donor will come from your world, and over time they will grow in their support of you.

Very rarely do donors start their relationship with anyone they want to support with a big check. There is usually a period of feeling out the cause they want to support. If their giving meets their goals and they feel as if their donation is being put to good use, donors will be prepared to make larger and larger gifts in time. Your big donors will come from your little donors, not from your efforts to get that one big check up front. To "play the lottery," so to speak, by placing your focus on finding that one big donor is to fail in working to building a community of supporters who will give more long term than that one-time "sugar daddy."

> **Fact:** There is a big-gift supporter out there for you. But you need to show *all* of your supporters how their gifts are benefitting your cause, and the big-gift supporter is far more likely to increase his or her gifts.

MYTH #4: THERE IS ONLY A FINITE POOL OF DONORS WHO WILL SUPPORT YOUR WORK/ DISCIPLINE/FIELD.

We can be deterred in our fundraising efforts because we believe we can only tap into the pool of donors who support work similar to the work we are doing. This is untrue.

I have witnessed, for instance, new theater companies all over the country starting off with this mindset. These companies believed they needed to get the people who support larger theater companies to support them. While there may be crossover between the two pools of supporters, your supporters will support you because of you and your particular vision, and they will come from your world and efforts.

For example, if you are a dance company, your donors will come from the people who bought tickets to your show or the families of the dancers performing in the show.

If you are a musician, you may find your donors from past show attendees, past album buyers, or among your neighbors.

Focus on your mission and efforts, and start to identify your potential supporters.

> **Fact:** Your constituents will be yours. Their various

relationships with anyone outside your sphere does not affect you.

MYTH #5: THE DONOR HAS A VERY FRAGILE PSYCHE.

This myth springs from the fear that if we ask someone for too much money (or ask at all) they will be offended. Or that if our solicitation letter is not perfect, they'll throw it in the trash. Or that if we don't hear from them, they are definitely not interested in supporting us. Or that because they said *no* once, they never want to support us ever again.

None of these assumptions or any of their variations are true. They are beliefs we create in our own minds and project onto donors. A client of mine recently went out on a limb to ask an old friend and supporter to make a lead gift for her upcoming campaign. After the conversation and the Ask, her friend said no to the amount. He did, however, thank her for thinking about him and encouraged her to keep on asking, even telling her when better times of the year were for him. He owned a series of restaurants and a lot of his money was tied up in the business. Donors can handle your Ask.

Fact: Donors are not that fragile.

MYTH #6: DONORS ARE SCARY.

Maybe you're noticing that fear is one of the great barriers in fundraising, and here it raises its head again. Many of us are actually afraid of our donors. We are afraid they will say *no*.

We are afraid we will overstep our bounds with them. Many of us fear reaching out to people for money.

Talking about money has become taboo. Money can be a touchy subject in our personal relationships. But this particular relationship, between the donor and the artist, involves the need for funds, and everyone knows it. It's not a secret that creative efforts need cash to make them real. Do not let fear of the donor hinder your ability or the need to ask for money.

Rest assured that donors are not to be feared. They are, in fact, some of the most passionate people out there, and they are very interested in us and our work. To use an old phrase, they are people who put their pants on one leg at a time, just like us.

> **Fact:** Donors are also wonderful people who will care enough to make a gift to support you, if you ask them.

MYTH #7: I HAVE TO DECEIVE OR TRICK A DONOR INTO GIVING.

We need to understand that donors give because they *want to*. Donors go through a process of thinking about their gift. Even if their giving seems to be by impulse to you, the donor made a conscious choice to give a gift to you.

Supporters give because they feel inspired. They give because their personal needs match your goals. You don't have to do anything but be honest about what you need and what you need it for. As long as you are true to your needs, you will find donors who want to support them. If you are dishonest about your efforts, you will not be able to keep donors. Eventually, their needs and your efforts will not match.

I have seen so many arts groups leave their true missions in order to chase down specific monies. For a long time, arts funding was geared toward supporting arts education in schools. Too many groups tried to create "educational" programs in an effort to get that money. The thinking was that it would help them support their main efforts. Unfortunately, these efforts almost invariably led to hard-to-manage programs and unsuccessful results in those educational programs. The money dried up, and the groups were back to square one in terms of focused, legitimate fundraising.

Fact: You don't need to trick donors and bend yourself out of shape to get funds.

SO, WHO ARE DONORS *REALLY?*

Donors believe in your work.

Donors have almost always participated in your work in one capacity or another before they give. Donors know who you are. Many have followed your growth and are interested in where you are going next. Many times these people follow you in spite of your lack of communication with them.

Donors want to see you or your project succeed,
and they want to know they helped.

That is to say, they sense and want more of a relationship with you and your work. Here's where the beauty of it lies: You are trying to accomplish something that requires money, and here comes a donor who *wants to* provide those funds. In you and your work, they have found a way they can help, and they're personally investing in order to see the idea succeed.

Donors share your vision of the world.

There are thousands of other creative people in the world, but your donors choose *you*. Something about what you are saying and doing resonates with them, otherwise why would they support you?

Donors need to give.

Why do they need to? Because of how good it makes them feel. Some want to be recognized publically, while some want to remain anonymous, but all of them want that great feeling that comes when they've helped to make something happen.

Donors come from all walks of life.

Some are wealthy and some are living paycheck to paycheck. Your donors share one thing however: a love of you and/or your work.

Donors want to feel close to you.

They give because it's their way of connecting. They want to hear from you, and they want to know about your vision, your creative process. Most of all, they want to feel they are a part of your artistic journey.

YOUR JOB NOW IS TO LEARN HOW TO *CONNECT* WITH THESE PEOPLE.

Your donors are already in your world. They really are. It's time to move misunderstanding and fear out of the way and *let* them support you.

Once you rid your mind of the myths about who donors are, you are already well down the pathway to raising the money you need.

Too many times I see fundraising fail, because the messaging only focuses on your needs. I need donations because I want to do this project. I need your gift because we are going through a tough time. Donate to us because we perform this particular function in our community. Over and over again, I see solicitations that follow one of these themes.

Now you know this is one-sided.

It's important that you start thinking *now* about the ways a donation can meet not only your needs but also the needs of your donor.

With that in mind, let's move ahead, and look carefully at how to apply this knowledge to the different aspects of fundraising.

3

MAKING THE CASE

IN THIS CHAPTER we will look at *why* you are asking, or making a case for a gift.

In marketing terms, this is called presenting the "value proposition," stating for your donor in clear terms what the resulting benefit will be when they give to you and your project or cause. Your fundraising efforts are going to be more successful when you learn how to do this.

Imagine a dance company that is running an experimental performance institute. Their purpose is to train future experimental artists. For years they have been running the program and curating classes for a very diverse range of students. They have also been offering scholarships to students who are a great fit for the accredited program, but who have already left school and can't fold the credits into their school packages. These scholarships came out of the dance company's operating expenses for years, and the coffers were never resupplied by enough income. So, basically, these scholarships were given at a loss to the company.

I use this as an illustration, because I was fortunate enough to work with a company that was in just such a position and started a fundraising effort for this kind of scholarship program.

As in every case, it's important to extend your thinking into the mind of potential donors. Here's how it works.

It would be a mistake to solicit funding by simply saying that the scholarships are a need and that donations are necessary. That plan of attack is not going to resonate deeply with people. Why? Because potential donors are very likely to have a multitude of questions about the program and the process. These questions may include:

> » Why should they support *these* students?
> » Aren't there already enough dancers in the world?
> » If other students are paying, why should someone receive a scholarship?

These and other questions are likely to be barriers inside the donor, causing them to hesitate or refrain from giving. For this reason, it's important to take yourself out of your perspective and put yourself into their perspective. **If you don't anticipate obstacles, you will not address them—and that makes for a weak Ask.**

So how do you enter into their perspective?

Start by asking yourself: What do I know that my donor does not know?

You may know, for example, that these students are special, and that they are the future of your field. Or you may know that bringing in the scholarship student is critical to the dynamic of the class, and that their participation will make everyone's participation more meaningful.

Here's the point: You know that these factors are vital to your program. Your donors are not likely to know any of these things *unless you tell them*. And so it is your task to think of the important questions donors might have, and tell them why their gift is important.

Here's another example.

Let's say you are an independent musician who needs to self-produce your first album. Self-production involves real costs, but the benefits of doing it may be huge. You'll have CDs to give to potential producers and promoters and something that you can share with your supporters to help build a following. You have been creating music for years, but you haven't documented it all in one place before.

These are the things you need to articulate to your potential supporters. Explain to them how their money will be used. Tell them how taking this step will help your growth as an artist and that it will help you advance your career. Let them know what goes into making an album. And most importantly, don't assume that your friend, supporter, or neighbor knows what it takes to make this happen. You are a music insider. Your supporters are most likely not. They likely don't understand the intricacies of creating an album, such as how long it takes to write a song, what goes into creating a CD, or how you come up with cover art. Even worse, they may have false visions of what it takes. Lay out the steps for them in clear and concise terms.

These are examples of how to make a case to a donor.

THE BEAUTIFUL PART

The beautiful part of this step in the process of fundraising is that you already know the answers to questions your donors are likely to have. You are passionate about what you do and have built your life around it. Now you just need to articulate what is inside you to others.

GETTING IT CLEAR IN YOUR OWN MIND

If you're a bit hazy on why you're asking for a donation, that is, what it will specifically do to help you or your project, it can be helpful to talk to other people not in your field. Particularly focus on those who are not closely related to your organization or your work, and explain to them why you are raising money. Encourage your associates to ask questions. Use their responses and your own to feed your messaging. Sometimes we are too caught up in our own perspective to see the issues that others will clearly see, and an outside perspective is always good when drafting an Ask.

Once, I received a wonderful solicitation in the mail. In it, the young artist creating her first solo show for a festival broke down exactly how she was going to use every amount of donated funds. A $500 donation would be used to pay for her sound designer, $100 would go toward costumes, and so on. I was excited by the overall concept of the show and felt like I knew very clearly how my gift was going to help. For that reason, I made a gift to that campaign.

This is a good place to mention that it is more than acceptable to ask donors to help pay you and your collaborators on a project. I have heard all too often that people are hesitant to ask for money to pay for their time on a project. Get over that. You're a creator and the driving force of the artistic work.

DONORS AND THEIR THINKING

Being specific and tangible in your campaigns will indeed help you. Donors want to know where their money is going and what it will accomplish. This is because donors want to support specific and tangible things. They want to know WHAT they are helping accomplish.

FOLLOW THROUGH . . . TO COMPLETION

Not only is it important to be specific in asking; it's very important to follow through.

Let's say an animal rescue organization has a dog in its care that needs specialized eye surgery. The organization goes out to its followers and asks for a donation to cover the costs of the procedure. One of its supporters steps up and makes the necessary gift. They are thanked profusely and publically, and the dog is rushed to the vet to have the procedure done. After the procedure is done, the rescue organization takes a photo of the dog and sends it on to the donor with a note saying that everything went well and the surgery was a success.

This exemplifies how you should follow through with what you said you would do with the money and let your donor(s) know that you did. Too often, this simple principle is ignored. Once you craft your Ask and go out and solicit a ton of money, it is a huge mistake to then do something different with those funds than you stated.

You must always do what you say you will do with the gift. An Ask needs to be honest in order to be good, and to have integrity is hugely important. Once a donor learns you have used their money for something other than what they gave it to you to accomplish, you can be sure you will not get another penny from them.

Let's say you do exactly what you proposed you would do with the gift. Tell the donor that. Close the loop. Make sure they leave with zero doubt that you did with their money what you said you would.

This is good fundraising practice and—not incidentally—gives you another reason to thank the donor for their gift.

A TEST-RUN

It's always a good idea to write out every aspect of your case to give before you do anything else with the Ask.

Pose and answer the potential questions you might get

from your supporters. Write down how you will use the money you bring in. Put everything down on paper, so that you will be ready to utilize any piece of the information when necessary. Use the document as a reference piece for when you are drafting a solicitation letter. Read it over before you go out for coffee with that potential supporter. Writing it down helps you remember it all. You may not use all of the reasons you wrote down in your Ask, but you will experience the confidence that comes from knowing your Ask is strong and factual. And a quiet confidence counts for *a lot*.

Once your case is made, it's time to sell it!

4

THE ASK

THE ONLY WAY to guarantee you won't receive a donation is if you don't ask. And failing to ask can be lethal to a cause or organization.

Recently, I watched an organization close its doors. Several years before the final demise of the institution, the local newspaper ran an article about the organization's struggles with the following quote: "One arts patron with millions to dispose of said, 'I haven't been asked to give'."

Organizations struggle financially, even to the brink of closure, because they simply do not ask for money. I have witnessed this lack of asking for support until it's too late be reenacted over and over and over again in organizations big and small. Small arts groups I have worked with put off the process of asking until they shoot out an email at the end of the year—or when someone's threatening to turn off the utilities—because they have to do *something*. Countless independent artists never seek help from their potential supporters at all.

As a result, worthwhile creative projects do not get funded; doors close and talented people can't quit their day jobs and do what they love.

The reasons behind not asking are plentiful, but the solution is simple:

Ask!

JUST ASK

A main goal of this book is to simplify the concept of fundraising. When exploring the actual process of asking for money, it's important to keep one thing in mind if nothing else: Simply doing it is light-years better than not doing it. Even a bad Ask has a chance to be successful—certainly over not asking.

Here, I'm reminded of an old joke.

A man prays, "O Lord, you know the mess I'm in. Please let me win the lottery."

The next week, he prays again. This time he's complaining. "O Lord, didn't you hear my prayer last week? I'll lose everything I hold dear unless I win the lottery."

The third week, he prays again, and now he's desperate. "O Lord, this is the third time I've prayed to you to let me win the lottery! I ask and I plead and still you don't help me!"

A booming voice resounds from heaven. "David, David, be reasonable. Meet me half way. Buy a lottery ticket!"

I'd even argue that there really isn't such a thing as a bad Ask. Only better ones. ("I did my part and bought the lottery ticket, Lord.")

What makes a good Ask? Here is a simple formulation.

WHAT

The first key component is that you need to be asking for *something*. Be very clear in *what* you're asking for money for.

Just approaching a potential donor and saying, "Can I have some money?" likely won't get you very far. A donor will want to know how you intend to use the money. How is their support going to be put to good use? What will it accomplish in real terms? As I said in an earlier chapter, donors want to help. Give them something tangible to help with.

The key word in there is tangible. Having said that, it is possible, for sure, that you can receive a donation simply to support your general work and your existence. Many groups run successful fundraising campaigns around the basic concept that they need support just to exist. Many of the most productive of these campaigns are successful simply because the organization has cultivated close relationships with their supporters over a long period of time, and if you treat your donors right, thank them properly, and make them feel a part of your efforts, you will have supporters who will give almost whenever asked. These people want to see you keep going.

Most of us, however, have not cultivated those relationships to the level that a supporter sees as a vital reason to keep them going. Sadly, this can even include people in their close circle of friends. If it's "give or I'll / we'll go under" and your donor doesn't see that as a problem or have some vested interest in the continuation of your work, you're *done*. And even threats of your imminent demise are unlikely to bring in the funds to sustain you.

As I said, a far more successful Ask is one in which you are asking for help with something tangible.

An animal shelter is going to have more success asking for money to help pay for an expensive procedure for cute little Mittens (picture with the big eyes included), than they will have asking for money because they have lots of unidentified kittens who need spay and neuter services.

A young theater company is going to have more success raising money to put on a specific show than they will fundraising for a season as a whole.

Again, this is because donors want to feel that they are helping to create something specific as opposed to something vague and general.

The hidden beauty of being specific and tangible in your Asks is that it opens up additional opportunities to ask. If you run a five-show season in your theater, you have five different shows for which you can seek support. Since you were so specific with your first Ask, you can confidently ask again for the next show. (It will help a great deal in the next Ask to mention that the previous show—the one they supported—came off because of their help.) Your supporters will understand your needs when you're specific, and can choose to support you again for another project.

Looking at it the other way around: If you start with a broad Ask, you narrow your ability to ask again. So, for example, if you ask for support for an entire season but then you were to go back for a specific show, you run the risk of a donor wondering what you did with their money the first time. Didn't it support *all* your shows? Where did that first contribution go? What was done with it?

Being specific, then, is the first key. When you are able to be specific and tangible, a donor has a stronger sense of how their support is being used and that their support made a real difference.

HOW

After you have settled on what you are asking for, you need to figure out *how* you are going to ask.

The concept is really simple. The more personal you can make the Ask, the better that Ask will be. Think of it this way:

Sitting in someone's living room and asking for their support is going to be more effective than sending a letter that they may toss out with the junk mail or set aside to "get to later."

Calling someone and asking for money, the next best thing, is still more personal and better than sending an email.

Sending someone an Ask by email ranks higher than asking in a general Facebook post.

The more intimately you connect with someone, the more success you will have.

As much as I might wish that all Asks be done face to face, not all fundraising campaigns can logistically happen with every Ask occurring across a table or over a cup of coffee or a glass of wine. It takes time and energy to connect with every person in your world one on one. Schedules have to be coordinated, timing has to work out, and a prior close connection in the relationship has to exist. (Let's face it, it's weird when someone you don't know well suddenly asks you to meet them somewhere for appetizers.)

For these reasons, you will want to look at your campaign in light of how you want to spend your energy. Here is a way you might focus your efforts.

If you are an independent artist raising a small amount from friends and family, then by all means make it personal and one on one.

For everyone else, take some time to plot out the value of each Ask and determine the best plan of attack individually.

Even if the person you're targeting as a higher-level donor is not a family member or close friend, asking someone for, say, $1,000, requires a different and more personal plan than asking someone for $25.

If you're asking for lower levels of funds—$25, $50, $100, or $200—a personal phone call or personalized note can work just as well.

The bottom line is, I recommend you think about what you're trying to raise, who you are asking, and how much you are asking for and plan accordingly.

EVEN BEFORE YOU ASK

It's a really good idea before asking to determine *the amount* for which you are going to ask.

Sure, you could send out a solicitation that isn't specific. Your donors will simply fill in whatever makes sense or feels comfortable to them—quite likely at the low end of that comfort zone. If you are raising money for something specific and tangible, however, you probably need a specific amount of money to make it work.

It is better (and easier) to prepare for an Ask by fully and carefully understanding what you need to raise and breaking that number into smaller amounts. Then you can assign those numbers to your different prospects. If you need $2,000 to purchase a new dance floor, you can break that down any number of ways. You might ask ten people to give you $200 or four people to give you $500. Whatever makes the most sense for your given base of donors should help you select the Ask amount.

The thing about asking for a specific amount if it's pinned to a tangible need is this: Most potential givers, even if they don't give the amount you ask for, will still give something. But if you *don't* ask for an amount, the likelihood you will get what you need is pretty slim.

I want to also emphasize here that it's okay to ask someone for more than you think they might feel comfortable giving. Donors won't be offended that you asked them for $1,000 when they only have the capacity to give $500. (Now, keep it within reason, of course. Remember that most everyday people cannot make $10,000 gifts!)

If possible, before selecting an amount, look at your donors' giving history. If they have traditionally given you $25 every year, that tells you something. (Maybe that $10,000 is a little ways away.) If they gave you $1,000 a couple years ago, but have only given $50 the last couple of years, that tells you something, as well. (Perhaps they aren't excited with your work or maybe that first Ask was really strong and effective, and you should revisit its message). Additionally, it never hurts to Google the donor or look at other organizations you know they support. Many organizations publically thank their supporters, which gives you a list of names and a rough giving amount. While giving to another organization does not necessarily correlate to what a donor will give to you, it can give you a picture of what they can afford.

WHO

Finally, of course, you will want to spend some time thinking about *whom* you are going to ask and how many people you need to ask.

As in the example of the $2,000 dance floor campaign I gave above, similar planning with any Ask can help you figure out how many people to approach for money and in what increments.

Let's say you need to raise that $2,000 and you decide you need ten people to give you $200. Do you have ten people in your world to approach for $200? But wait: Even if you went out right now and asked those ten people, that's probably not enough. The reality is that not everyone you ask is going to give. Don't get bent out of shape. People —even people who are close to, like, and would support us if they could—say no for a wide variety of reasons. (They have a surprise repair payment that month. They are in between jobs. They just gave to someone else, and so on.) You need to plan ahead for the likelihood of turn-downs.

Personally I use a "Rule of Four." For every gift I want to get, I have to ask four people, with the expectation that three will say no. You can certainly start with the same formula or develop your own based on your experiences. Whatever you do, just be sure to take into account the likelihood of getting "no" for an answer.

I can't emphasize this point enough, because adjusting expectations lowers your level of disappointment (and irritation), and that makes it very liberating. You WILL hear no. You'll hear it a lot. And to know in advance that it very likely has nothing to do with you personally and probably more to do with the supporter and their situation can free you from the tangles of self-doubt and negative emotional responses on your part. Knowing it will happen, knowing people close to you may not respond, and accommodating for it in advance, makes the inevitable comfortable.

DO IT

Now that you know what you are asking for, how you are going to ask, have a sense of the amount to ask for, *and* know who you are going to ask, there is only one more thing left to do: Ask!

Lots of publications show you how to work through all the minutia of the absolutely perfect Ask, whether it's in writing or in person. I won't replicate their valiant efforts of crafting the perfect letter or scripting the perfect meeting. Just know for certain there is no such thing as perfect, and the uniqueness of every Ask makes perfection irrelevant.

What I want to offer are simple but important things to keep in mind, regardless of how you ask.

First: Don't "bury the lead," as they warn in news-speak. When your goal is to ask for money, get to the point.

If you have a one-hour meeting scheduled with a potential donor, then sure, open with some small talk, but get to the Ask well before minute 55 of the conversation. If you are writing fundraising letters, it's okay to open with some background information, but don't bury the actual Ask on the second page of the letter. Put it up front where people can see it.

Donors can feel set up if you take a long time—and feel like you're "buttering them up"—when you beat around the bush in asking for money.

Second: An Ask is an Ask. Don't clutter it with other goals.

If you are asking for money, *just* ask for money. Do not also try and sell tickets to a show.

If you're asking for money for a specific project, don't waste time talking about another project. If other projects need help, there will be time to ask for help with them. You have an immediate and pressing need that requires attention now.

Keep your current Ask clear and focused.

Finally: Remember to come from a place of confidence.

Be positive about yourself, your project, and your goals, and the person you are asking will pick up on that energy. This dynamic needs to hold true when meeting in person, in a phone call, in a letter, or in an email. Remember, you need to believe more than anyone in what you are doing, and no one can present that passion, excitement, and energy better than you.

On the flip side: Remember that your problems are not the donor's problem. Your donors did not get you into the financial position that requires $20,000 or you will have to close. Even in situations that are stressful and dire (and there are many worthy of fundraising for), stay focused on the positives. Sure, there's an immediate issue, but how is that donor's support going to get you through it? How will their donation ensure that you never get into that position again? How are they helping you reach beyond this tough time?

MAKE IT EASY

Before you go out there and start asking, be sure you have thought through how your donor can give to you and your cause and that all the possible ways are easy. I have on multiple occasions attempted to make donations to different groups only to get frustrated when I'm not able to find a donation link on their website. Why are they making it so hard for me to give them money?

Think through how *you* can accept donations (check by mail, online, over the phone with credit card, and so on) and communicate those methods clearly to your donor. Try to set up systems with the fewest barriers between your donor and you. If you mail a solicitation, put a reply envelope in with the letter. Better yet, self-address and put a stamp on it so all your donor has to do is write down their credit card info or write a check and drop it in the mail. Have your donation link on the main page of your website so your donor doesn't have to dig through the site to find the place to give. Are you sending a solicitation email? Have the link they click to donate go directly to the place they enter their credit card information.

Now all that's left is to go out there and ask for money, and ask often. The more you ask, the more comfortable you will be with it. Like any activity, the more you practice, the better you will get, the more comfortable you will be, and the more successful you will become. Push yourself past your initial barriers and I promise that you will get to a place of comfort and confidence.

5

THANK YOU

IN MY HUMBLE OPINION, the most important phase of fundraising, hands down, is the Thank You.

If you can learn how to thank people properly, you will have great success in your current and future efforts.

Unfortunately, the Thank You is usually put on the back burner. It's the last phase of the asking process, and that makes it both the last one we think about and the first one we're most likely to forget altogether. Or do poorly.

AS ALWAYS, SIMPLE IS BEST

I have been employed by large arts organizations that make saying "thank you" a complex process. A gift will come in and be registered by one of the more junior people in the Development Department. Then there will be a delay in creating a thank-you letter because they want enough gifts to come in to create a bulk mailing. Then a person higher up in the organization needs to review the thank-you letter before it can move forward. Finally, the head of the organization needs to find time to sign the letters. Before you know it, weeks or months have passed since the gift was received from the donor.

I have seen young artists put a ton of effort into their fundraising campaigns for one of their early projects. They exude passion and excitement to their audiences and followers, and that enthusiasm translates into many small gifts for their effort. By the time they meet their goal and move forward with their project, though, they have expended so much energy. As a result, they post a quick "thank you" to all their supporters on Facebook and get to work making their project a reality.

I have watched small organizations stop gathering phone numbers for their supporters and even stop entering in addresses to their databases during a fundraising campaign. They know they have their supporters' emails and when their campaign is done, they can email them all a PDF of their official thank-you and tax deduction letter, as if that's all that's required or needed.

Each of these examples cause future fundraising efforts to suffer, because organizations do not understand why the Thank You is such a priority. For this reason, it's important to focus on it here.

WHAT MAKES A GOOD THANK YOU?

There are two main things to keep in mind when thanking people.

The first is *timeliness* or *speed.*

The second is *sincerity.*

Timeliness

If nothing else, if you can respond to a gift quickly and express your appreciation honestly, you will see major returns for your efforts.

A Thank You should reach the donor as soon as you can after you receive a gift. Think about the act of giving from a donor's perspective and you will understand why. When a donor chooses to make a gift, they are making a deeply personal and emotional decision. They get a solicitation that speaks to them in a powerful way. They consciously decide they want to help, and to do that, they write a check or enter their credit card information with an amount of money that has meaning to them. They send this gift off to you and then they wait. Their energy is high because they feel really good about what they just did. Giving can even be a euphoric feeling for some people. Writing out that check can be exciting and filled with passion for what they want to support.

What happens the longer you wait to say thanks for their gift?

At first, the donor may not notice. They know it takes some time for the mail to arrive or for an organization to get to their gift. There is a grace period unique to each donor, determined by their personal expectations. After some period, however, each donor will start to wonder if his or her gift ever got there at all. They wonder if maybe their check was lost in the mail or perhaps there was a problem with their credit card. At some point, they will see that the check has cleared their account or the gift amount has shown up on their statement.

After they know you have taken their money, they will start to wonder why you haven't said anything or acknowledged them yet. With each day that passes, you take the chance that the donor will feel unappreciated or even irritated that you have said nothing. The longer you wait to say "thank you," the more likely you are to damage a relationship before it has even gotten started.

All too often, when the thank-you letter does finally arrive in the donor's mail, it's a form letter. It thanks them for their gift, but the letter is clearly the same letter sent to everyone who donates. The messaging is generic, the signature is clearly scanned in, and the only reference to them is their name on the envelope or perhaps on the address line of the page.

This leads us to the need for. . ..

Sincerity

Add a lack of sincerity on top of a slow "thank you" and you have done damage to a relationship that was born from such a beautiful place, one where the giver *used to* feel such a part of your vision, you art, your project, and your passion.

Now they feel like an after-thought, or just a means to an end.

The good news is, it doesn't take much to avoid this type of scenario. With a little planning and focus from the beginning of your fundraising process, you can get meaningful thank-you letters or notes out *fast*.

HERE'S HOW YOU DO IT

Start by thinking through the different ways you can express your appreciation.

The most meaningful way to say "thank you" is face to face, if that's possible. Make it a point to visit with your donor, look them in the eyes, and tell them how much it meant to you to receive their gift. One-on-one interaction is a very powerful thing. Sure, the down-side is that it might take too much time or coordination to be in the same place at the same time with your donor.

If at all possible, try to see your donor shortly after their gift arrives and offer them a personal "thank you."

Another meaningful way to accomplish this is to *call* your donor. Calling someone is becoming less and less commonplace in our society. Many of us do not even think of our phones as phones anymore. In a world where we make fewer and fewer phone calls and send more texts and emails, the phone "thank you" is still deeply personal and meaningful. You can express in your own words, directly to your donor, how much their gift meant.

The great thing is it takes almost no effort to pick up the phone and dial a donor's number almost immediately after you've received their gift. Imagine the pleasant surprise it will be for the donor to hear from you—maybe even before they think the gift got there.

I learned the importance of this simple act by routinely calling donors the minute their gift crossed my desk. It was so easy and natural to say "thank you" over the phone. Even if I got a voicemail, I would leave a message saying I had received their gift and what it meant to me. They didn't even have to call me back if they didn't want to, but they knew I received their gift and that it was highly valued.

Like the phone call, the handwritten note seems to have become an art form from a bygone era. We are so used to sending people emails now that most of us no longer write actual letters. It feels as though the only mail we get any more are bills and credit card offers. But a handwritten note can make a huge impact on the recipient. Getting a personalized letter from the head of the organization you just wrote a check to can be a delightful surprise that will resonate with them for a long time.

I highly recommend one of the methods above before you resort to sending your donor an email. These days we are buried in emails. Once an email has left the viewable portion of your inbox, it has a tendency to leave your mind, as well.

If you need to email your "thank you" or want to send an email in addition to a letter or call:

First, make sure the email comes directly from the email of a person on staff and not through an email marketing system such as Constant Contact or Mail Chimp. Preferably, have the highest-level person in the organization send the email. Draft it for them if you have to and if it will speed up the process of getting it out. For you one-man shops, this will be easy; for larger organizations, it's too easy to have an intern send out a thank-you email. Ideally, the email will come from the person who actually asked for the money from the donor.

Second, personalize the email as much as you can. It's too easy to create one template and cut-and-paste it for each donor. Fight against this. Remember that every donor is unique, and your response to him or her should feel the same.

Remember, too, that an automatic response from the company processing their credit card is not a thank-you email. Don't think just because they got an email instantaneously when they hit "submit" online that this is the same thing as you saying "thank you" in any other way. We expect an immediate response from a system, and it has little meaning with us anymore.

After email, there is also the old-fashioned thank-you letter at your disposal. This can be a powerful document. I have seen it abused so often that I am placing it toward the end of my list. Too often, as I've mentioned, the thank-you letter becomes a form letter devoid of meaning and passion. It becomes a box to be checked while going through the end stages of the fundraising process.

I strongly encourage you to see your donor, call your donor, write them a note, or even email your donor properly before you send out your thank-you letter. This way you can take the time needed to compose the letter and feel like you have already connected with your donor quickly and meaningfully.

As for the thank-you letter itself, it can be great, if you follow these guidelines:

» Personalize the letter as much as you can. As noted above with the thank-you email, don't write just one letter and send it to everyone.

» Thank the donor(s) by name. There is no place for "Dear friend," or "Dear donor," when starting a thank-you letter.

» Make the letter come from the highest person in the organization, preferably from whomever the Ask came from originally.

» Always, always sign the letter. With ink. Probably a different color from the ink printed on the letter. This shows people that a human is actually saying "thank you."

» Even better, have the person who is signing the letter also write a personal note on it.

» Get that letter in the mail as soon as you can! Don't delay.

Finally, let's circle back and touch again on the Thank You by social media. More and more I am seeing groups thank their supporters online. It's very easy to send out a tweet or post a Facebook comment to thank donors for a gift.

I would be very hesitant to do this for a couple of reasons. You don't know necessarily if the donor wants to be singled out publically or even wants their friends and connections to know. You also don't know if the person will even see it. Not everyone checks their accounts regularly, so you may be creating a situation where you feel you have thanked someone when in reality they might never know.

Yes, there are a few scenarios in which a social media

Thank You can be appropriate. I recommend you limit these to specific online campaigns, targeted to a specific community and where the potential supporters know ahead of time that they will be thanked in this way (and ideally have the ability to opt out when making the gift). Regardless, I would still recommend that even if you do thank your donors in this way, you also pick another more personal method to accompany it.

IN ADVANCE

Before you even ask for money from anyone, take time to sketch out how you are going to say "thank you." That way when the gifts start rolling in, you are not playing catch up with your "thank yous." Choose the methods that make the most sense for you, and dedicate yourself to the process.

When setting up your thank-you process, here are some important things to keep in mind.

Keep your "thank yous" focused on thanking your donor.

Do not give into the inevitable urge to get something into your Thank You that doesn't belong. It's easy to think that you are saving your time and the time of the donor by combining messages. I have seen people, for example, promote their next show in their thank-you letter and then ask for another gift. Avoid doing this. It takes away from the sincerity of the Thank You. All that should be in your contact is "thanks!"

This is also highly important: If you asked them from something specific in your solicitation, then reference that in your Thank You. This helps the donor feel like you are true to what you have asked for. The worst thing you can do is ask someone for help purchasing a new dance floor and when you thank them for their gift you tell them you're using the money for salaries. A Thank You is an extension of your Ask and is a critical part of the giving continuum (Ask, Thank, Communicate). The end of the process needs to be done in context with the purpose of the Ask.

Make your Thank You meaningful. The deeper you can express your appreciation, the more of a positive impression it will make. If you asked for money, it was for an important reason. You needed help making something happen. It was important enough that you felt other people would be compelled to support. So, express that deep, meaningful appreciation in your Thank You. If you don't express the love, admiration, and joy that you feel, how are they to know how much their gift meant?

A VERY PERSONAL EXPERIENCE

While I was dealing with my wife's illness, I poured myself into crafting a vision of the future and a fundraising campaign to support that vision for the arts center I was working for at the time. It was a change for the company and a risk for me personally. The problem was, I was the new guy in a very old organization. I risked irritating some of the longtime supporters with my new ideas and plans. While I worked hard to build internal buy in, I never knew if I was really reaching others in a meaningful way.

Shortly after I launched the campaign, I received a check from one of the most loyal supporters of the center. The amount was twice what I had asked for. I immediately picked up the phone to call her and while leaving a message on her voicemail, I started crying. I was so thankful and relieved by her generosity I couldn't keep my feelings in. The weight of all the stress in my life simply overcame me.

I promise you that neither she nor I will ever forget that message. I don't necessarily advocate you cry tears of joy every time you get a gift, but be sure to be honest in your thanks and true to how you feel. Donors really are moved by sincerity.

If the gift was truly meaningful, you can never say "thank you" enough.

When I was building Washington, D.C's first Fringe Festival, I was in charge of raising the necessary funds. I had built a small database of followers for the project and decided to mail out a solicitation letter. The first check that came in was from an individual I had never met in person. I wrote a thoughtful thank-you note and sent it off as fast as I could. That woman's name will always be emblazoned in my mind. I was never able to meet her face to face during my time with the organization, though we definitely traded many communications, but I met her many years later after I had left that organization. Even then, I made it a point to tell her how appreciative I was for that first gift.

While saying "thank you" at that time served no specific or immediate purpose, I know that if I am ever in need of a gift from her in the future for another project, she will remember that I made a point of reiterating my thanks years after the original gift.

Keep it short and sweet. It doesn't take a lot to say thank you. It is, after all, just two words. While conveying your sincere appreciation, you may be struck with the urge to talk more about the project, what activities you have lined up in the near future, and how your vision for the project has grown. While these are all important things to share with your supporters at some point, they can all too often cloud your initial goal of saying thank you. Keep your messages focused. Know your task and stick to it. If you want to follow up with more information later, go ahead. It's great to keep people informed. Just keep your Thank You a "thank you."

I began this chapter by saying: The most important phase of fundraising, hands down is the Thank You.

It's the most important part because it will have the greatest impact on your future fundraising success. I have seen poorly written and badly timed solicitations still bring in money. It's the Thank You that can determine whether that donor will ever give again and if so, how much. Use this often overlooked step in the fundraising process as an opportunity, not only to close the Ask, but as a way to build good will for the future.

By saying "thank you" quickly and meaningfully, you only make it easier on yourself the next time you ask for money. The donor will remember you and how good you made them feel and will be more inclined to give again or give more. Your first Ask for money will likely not be your last, so set yourself up on the path for future success.

6

CULTIVATION

ONE OF THE CORE elements of fundraising is building a strong connection with your donors. In my experience with organizations and artists, it is often overlooked or undervalued.

For that reason, this chapter focuses on cultivating your relationship with current and potential supporters—or the art of **relating** to them when you are not asking for money.

I live outside of Washington, D.C., and have always been deeply engaged in politics. So, naturally, I started getting involved in campaigns and supporting my local politicians with donations.

On my last birthday I received a call from a number I didn't recognize, so I let it go to voicemail. When I finally listened to the voicemail, I found out the call was from my Congressman wishing me a happy birthday. It was a totally cool message and it was a blast sharing it with my friends. Now, I don't believe that he actually cared that it was my birthday, and I am certain that a staff member just gave him a card with my name and phone number on it (along with a handful of other people who had birthdays or other special events going on), and said: "Call him." Doesn't matter. The call made me feel recognized and appreciated, and I am more likely to make another donation to a future campaign because of the outreach.

This is a case in point as to why it's important to reach out sometimes when you don't need something.

I've already highlighted the importance of the Thank you. That one small part of the process makes a world of difference, because in one beautiful, proactive step you acknowledge the donor, make them feel important, and do it without any expecting something in return.

A lot of goodwill is generated when you turn your focus onto your donors and validate them. And that in itself is hugely important. Connecting with people when you don't need money from them is a practice you should be mindful of doing regularly. If you only talk to your supporters when you need something, you are going to make them feel as if all they are for you is a bank account.

Organizations big and small fall into the poor habit I call, "communicate only when we need something." Newsletters are begrudgingly created and sent so infrequently they come across like an afterthought. In many organizations the only letters that go out to donors are Asks. Independent artists run a big campaign and then disappear into the world to create their masterpiece, never reaching out again to the people who supported them, who are left to wonder what happened to their donation or the artist they cared about.

The beautiful thing is that the solution to this deficit in communication is completely easy: Make a simple plan to reach out to people when you're *not* asking them for money.

All right, I get it:

» You're too busy
» You don't know what to say
» You don't want to bother people

Well, let's push past those barriers, because doing so is crucial for the long haul.

First, let's consider the possibility that you are too busy. I do understand. You are underfunded, short staffed, and have your own work to do. But if you want to get past being underfunded, want to hire more staff, or need the space to focus, raising more money will assist you with all of that. You get more money by building a better pool of supporters.

With this in mind, do you see how vital it is for you engage in the practice of reaching out to your donors and planning it into your schedule?

You can start this by setting up a simple process, one to which you can dedicate yourself. Certainly, whatever plan you create needs to work for you. The more comfortable and realistic the process, the more likely you will be to follow it.

Here are some examples of general ways you can reach out when not asking for money:

» Ask supporters for advice and thoughts on a topic or idea. "What do you think about me exploring this idea?"

» Express gratitude or appreciation for some connection you had with them. "It was great seeing you at x event" or "I really appreciate your help with x, y, and z."

» Share with them news from your broader community. "Did you see our sister company is doing x next week?"

» Share thoughts and musings from recent travel or tour. "When I was in Italy I thought a lot about how the Italians support the arts. I wanted to share that with you."

» Send exciting photos when you have them. "We just did a photo shoot for our next show. Check out how awesome the team looks."

» Share an interesting anecdote. "We had a very interesting conversation at our school today."

» Express to your supporters when you feel excited. "We just got nominated for the local magazine awards. I couldn't wait to let you know."

Use these types of events as triggers to reach out to your list of contacts. The next time something is interesting to you, think about if it might be interesting to others and start reaching out about it.

I'll illustrate for you the simplest process I can think of to set up a non-solicitation communication system.

Buy a bunch of index cards (any size will do), and a box for them to go into. (Honestly, a rubber band will work as well. The goal is to keep all the index cards together.) On each index card write the name, phone number, and email of one of your donors or special supporters. Put those cards in whatever order you want.

Then when something exciting happens with your work—let's say you received your first big grant—take the card on top of the stack and call or email that person with the exciting news. Move that card to the bottom of the stack, and call or email the next person. Keep going as far as you can go, always moving the person you just contacted to the back of the stack and moving on to the next person. Some days you will be able to get through the entire stack of names. Other days you might only be able to get through a few. It doesn't matter. What matters most is that eventually you will touch everyone you need to touch.

There's always exciting news or developments with a project your supporters funded. You only need to let the exciting events in your world trigger an impulse to reach out to someone. People who support you want to share in your excitement, and if your system is simple enough and fits well into your life, you will be able to connect with them in deeply meaningful ways that make them feel connected to you. After all, you cared enough about them to call and share good news.

I illustrated this concept with a deck of index cards. I can't think of anything easier. You can replicate that idea, however, in whatever way makes the most sense to you. Maybe you love using a certain computer program. Perhaps there's a mobile application you like and can use for this purpose. Maybe you are equipped with the latest development and fundraising software. It doesn't matter what you use or how you do it.

What matters is that you commit to this as a regular process.

I want to encourage you here to work on being as honest and sincere as you can be with your communications. Everything I have listed can easily become carefully edited marketing or grant copy. While that can be fine, it won't resonate as powerfully with a donor as a message that is honest and comes from the heart. I started this book by sharing with you my own personal and tragic story. I didn't have to. I could have kept the language focused on fundraising concepts and nothing more. However, it's these moments of transparency that create real connections with people.

In the end, it's just important that you talk to your supporters. And as with the Ask, the more intimate you can make your non-Ask conversation, the more powerful it will be. The act of talking to a donor by any means when not asking for money will move you far ahead of hundreds of other people and groups in their estimation. And making a phone call to tell them about the progress of the project to which they donated will raise you to the stratosphere in terms of connection with them.

IT'S SO SIMPLE TO DO

Yes, it's that easy. Even if you don't consider yourself a "people person," just pick up the phone and call the donor. Sometimes barriers are just in our heads. This leads me to the third barrier you may need to overcome: You don't want to bother people.

Guess what: You won't. If a person can't talk on the phone, they won't answer. Leave a cheerful voicemail telling them what you wanted to say and letting them know there's no need to call back unless they'd like to hear more information. Then move on to the next person. Maybe the person you called sounds super busy. Quickly get out your message and invite them to call you another time or email you if they want to learn more.

Of course, you can always send the one-on-one email. The donor will read it when they have the time and may never respond. It's all good.

Whatever you do to reach out, you will be moving ahead with the important process of showing your donors that you really care about them. It may be foreign to them at first. **Few people are doing this.** Even fewer are doing it with any consistency. Your efforts to communicate more often and when you are not "selling" anything will make you stand out in a world filled with people and organizations that don't. I promise, though, that your supporters will get over the foreign feeling created by your efforts and quickly come to welcome it. They will start to recognize your number and gladly take the call and chat longer and longer. They may start calling and emailing back.

I remember in one of my roles making a conscious effort to reach out regularly. The first time I would reach people and say, "Hello, I'm Damian Sinclair from x organization," I could palpably feel the unease on the other end of the line. They were bracing themselves for what had to be an Ask. When I expressed what I needed to and wished them a beautiful night, I could tell they were surprised and relieved. The more I did it, the warmer the conversations became.

The point is that you and your donor will be more and more engaged in good communication. And a more engaged donor is going to give and support more often *and* is very likely to give more.

CONCLUSION

Why not sit down now and use the ideas in this chapter, plus others that will come to you, to create a list of ways you plan to stay in occasional and important touch with your supporters. Then take time to schedule when and how that will happen.

You're building a foundation for a lasting connection.

7

FUNDRAISING DATA AND TOOLS

YOU CAN FUNDRAISE with nothing more than paper, a pencil or pen, stamps and envelopes, a phone, and an email account. Seriously. It's no more complicated than that.

Complications arise when we get hung up on the tools and trappings of fundraising. Fancy fundraising software, expensive packets and letterhead, elaborate benefits for giving, professionally designed videos: These things certainly can enhance a fundraising campaign, but they are only tools.

As you continue with your preparations, it's important to remember that fundraising is simple.

You don't need a lot of stuff to do it, just some simple know-how. You cultivate your supporters, make a case for a donation, ask for the money, and thank people. You don't need to do anything more than that. So, be cautious before you jump into anything more complicated or with an expense attached to it.

COLLECTING DATA

One of the important functions you'll need to be ready prepare for is the collection of data. In fact, you'll want to collect as much data as you can. It will tell you what worked, what didn't, and how to make choices moving forward. Collecting data will allow you to remember conversations and track giving. Here is just the start of the information you will want to track.

DONOR INFORMATION

Try to record as much donor data as you can, such as:

- » Full name
- » Address
- » Phone number
- » Email address
- » Marital status
- » Spouse's name
- » Children's names
- » Birthdate

Seems simple, right?

It's a mistake to trust our memories to hold on to this information. Don't. Document it and store it in a place where you can find it. Don't depend on memory for anything fundraising related. You may not be able to recall it when you need it most.

Also, try to gather as much as you can, even if you don't plan on using it. I can't tell you how many times I work with a new client only to find out that they never collected addresses for their supporters. The response I get as to why is almost universal: "We have their email address and don't mail anything."

I've mentioned already, and say it again for emphasis, that a handwritten note or letter can be powerful—far more powerful than an email. One reason to capture addresses is that even if you never send a supporter a piece of mail, you can get so much more information just by having an address on file.

For example, by collecting addresses you can perhaps learn the locale where most of your supporters are from. Does everyone come to your shows from the same zip code? Well, then perhaps it makes great sense to spend some time, energy, and resources in that zip code, as opposed to one where no one in your audience comes from.

DONATION INFORMATION

Tracking your gifts is extremely important. As is true with donor information, you never know when you'll need this kind of detail, and if you just commit it to memory you may not be able to recall it, or you may remember inaccurately.

Here are details you're wise to collect:

» Date the gift was received

» Amount of the gift

» What campaign the gift was for

» How the gift made was made (by credit card, check, online)

» What the check number was

» Date you sent a Thank You

» Whether a note came with the gift, and what it said

This kind of important detail will be hard to remember without documentation. When you gather this information religiously, it will help you inform future efforts.

For example, you can easily identify the people who regularly give you money. Maybe this can guide you to spend a little more time with a specific person. If you see that a person gives the same amount every time you ask, maybe it's time to ask for a little more. At the very least you need to know what people have historically given, so that you can track your success in fundraising, as well as your overall progress.

FUNDRAISING CONVERSATIONS

One of the most overlooked parts of data collection is documenting the conversations you have had with your supporters. We think we will remember a conversation or that we won't need to remember what was talked about. The reality is, most of us won't remember, and the details of past conversations with a supporter can prove extremely helpful with future conversations.

Now, I'm not recommending that you take notes during your conversations with supporters. This would be distracting and keep you from fully engaging in the moment. I do suggest, however, that you get the information from the conversation down as soon as possible after the interaction. The more time you wait, the less reliable your memory will be.

Here are some of the things you will want to take notes on from your interactions with supporters.

» Simply that an interaction happened

» When the conversation occurred

» Where it took place (on the phone, in person, in a restaurant, in someone's home or office)

» What you talked about

» What the supporter talked about

» What they said that caused you to think, "I should remember that"; say, a child's birthday or an important life event such as an anniversary or an upcoming trip, or a health issue

» A preference toward any part of your work that they expressed

» Something that troubled them about their life, politics, a social issue, your work

» Anything you promised them, such as a brochure or other follow-up information

» Anything they promised to do for you, such as bring their friends to your next show, or make an introduction to the head of their organization or company or to the owner of an important venue

The point I want to impress on you is this: Document as much as you can, because you never know when you might need the information. Get it down when it's fresh in your mind and file it away. The next time you meet with that supporter, you will have a great set of data to draw from. You can read over your notes and let them guide the new conversation. (If they said they were highly allergic to shellfish, then it's probably not a great idea to suggest you meet at Red Lobster.) Maybe they said they would introduce you to someone and haven't made good on that offer yet. Now you can remind them.

CORRESPONDENCE

It's also important to keep track of your correspondence with your supporters. This documentation will help you create a full picture of your communications with a supporter.

> » Were they on your email list when you sent that update?

> » Did you send them a solicitation letter?

> » Did you send them a thank-you note?

> » Did you call them? When? At what time?

If you can, keep copies of the letters you sent them. File away your email correspondence. Track your phone calls. Mark down whatever you can, because it paints a complete picture of how you interact with your supporters.

TOOLS FOR RECORD KEEPING AND DATA RETRIEVAL

Tools should be used to enhance your efforts and make the process easier for you. But remember that the tool itself does not fundraise. Your energy, efforts, and passion are what are truly effective in getting the job done.

I'm not "anti tool" by any stretch. I use several different fundraising software packages for my clients and multiple different computer programs to track critical information. I have clients all over the country and dozens of simultaneously running campaigns. The tools I use help me get the job done for my clients more efficiently and allow me to maintain a large amount of data quickly. Having said that, I could still do it with just pen and paper. Nothing about fundraising is so complex that you *need* to use anything more than your know-how and personal touch.

A tool can help you, for example, to record important data. People can try to sell you on the idea that you need expensive or technologically advanced modes of record keeping. Not so.

How you choose to record this information is up to you. You need to pick the system that you will use (if you don't use the tool it can't work for you), and that matches your needs. You can get 100 3x5 index cards for under $2 or fancy, cloud-based fundraising software for $300/month.

Maybe you have thousands of potential supporters. Pick the development software. Maybe you are just getting started and only have friends and family to reach out to. Pick the index cards.

I'm not going to recommend specific tools for you to use; there are many options out there and everyone's needs are unique and specific. I just want to reiterate that whatever you choose, pick a system that you will be comfortable with and will use regularly. If you are a note taker, buy a bunch of notebooks and use them to collect specific information. If you love computers, research the software that is best for you and your personal needs. Remember, bigger and more expensive does not necessarily make it better for you.

If you find yourself not using a tool that you selected, scrap it and move on to something else right away. Don't force something that isn't working, but **do** force yourself to keep track of information.

To this point, we've focused on data collection in which you can and should engage if you want to be successful at bringing in funds. Now I want to touch on another tool that has become popular, and offer some perspective and cautions.

CROWDFUNDING

While I am not interested in providing an exhaustive list of different fundraising tools, I do want to spend some time on one in particular, and that's crowdfunding systems such as Kickstarter, Indigogo, Hatchfund, and Pledgemusic.

These systems are just that: tools. **They don't replace the personal collection of data and the very important need for connection you can build with your donors. Nothing can replace that.**

Crowdfunding has been around for a very long time and basically consists of getting a lot of gifts from as many people as possible using an individual's networks and connections. In fact, as far back as 1885, Joseph Pulitzer used his newspaper *The New York World* to help collect 160,000 donations to pay the more than $100,000 required to build the base for the Statue of Liberty.

We hear stories like these, and it's tempting to think: *Maybe I need to do this—even if it doesn't suit my style.*

Hold on.

The rise of the Internet age has led to the quick growth of crowdfunding platforms to raise money for projects of all types. We have witnessed an explosion of the number of people using crowdfunding systems to raise money for artistic projects. Some have been more successful than others.

As I said, these systems, while appealing, are simply tools to accomplish certain functions of the fundraising process. To raise money successfully and consistently, you cannot use any tool to replace the core beliefs that I lay out in this book. All too often I have seen crowdfunding systems replace the dedicated personal work required to successfully raise money in the long term.

Here are some things to be aware of if you choose to run

a crowdfunding campaign and why they can potentially do more harm than good.

OVER-FOCUS ON REWARDS

One of the things that is off-putting to me about crowdfunding is that it encourages an over-dependence on giving benefits or rewards at different levels of giving. Donating money carries its own rewards for the donor, which we cover in this book. An overreliance on giving the donor something in return for his gift shifts the act of donation from giving to transaction and thus distances the donor and their support from you and your work.

BOMBARDMENT WITH COMMUNICATION

A core function of many of these systems is to raise a certain amount by a certain date. While inherently this is not a bad thing (I'm a firm believer that fundraising should have tangible goals), I have seen it devolve into some bad habits. I can't tell you how many people I have wanted to unfollow on Facebook or Twitter during the last week of their campaigns. Their posts and urgency become more frequent and greater, and for some supporters this can be very off-putting.

LESS PERSONAL

Many crowdfunding campaigns are run in ways that remove all personal interactions between artist and potential supporter. You put out a video on the site and people either watch it or don't. You're missing a beautiful opportunity to truly connect with a potential supporter: The give-and-take that informs future conversations and builds long-lasting relationships.

LETS PEOPLE OFF EASY

I think much of the appeal of crowdfunding is that you do not have to directly ask any one person for money. This means that you don't have to ask any one person for anything in particular. You cast a wide net and take anything that comes in as long as the end result is the same. In many cases, the people who give to these campaigns give less than what they are capable of giving. Had you done a little bit of homework and reached out to that person independently, you might have been able to receive twice as much money to support your project.

BAD HABITS

These systems can develop some very bad habits, especially with people just starting down the fundraising road. I have seen inarticulate case statements (why should someone give), lack of gift follow-through, no deep appreciation or thanks to individual donors, and poor tracking of donor information. Maybe you can get away with all or some of this in your first successful campaign, but these are not habits that will lead to prolonged success in fundraising.

I haven't come here to try to bury crowdfunding systems, only to highlight potential pitfalls of using them. Mainly, if you do decide to use a crowdfunding tool, never forget that it's just a tool. As such, its benefits are:

» Quick and easy communication

» Ability to help you reach a broader audience

» Ability to let supporters promote your efforts more widely

With any tool you use, never let it get in the way of the core principles of fundraising laid out in this book. With proper planning and execution, a crowdfunding system could complement your campaign efforts nicely.

Now let's look at another tool.

FUNDRAISING EVENTS

Yes, fundraising events like galas, charitable shows, casino nights, and so forth are simply fundraising tools and not fundraising itself. Events can be powerful tools to make connections with your donors and give them a fun and fulfilling way to expand their financial support. They can be great marketing tools for an organization and can bring more and more new people into the organization's fold.

However, fundraising events can be large and cumbersome activities requiring a lot of personal and staff/volunteer time to implement. Before you venture down the path of starting an event, make sure you take time to quantify its costs versus potential rewards. More often than not, your time will be better spent simply asking donors for support and not hiding that Ask within an event.

Remember: A fundraising tool is just a device that aids in the implementation of a task—it is not a replacement for the task. Fundraising is simple enough at its core. To do it, you don't need anything more than paper, a pencil or pen, stamps and envelopes, a phone, and an email account.

And your very personal touch.

8

INSTITUTIONAL GIVING

IT MUST BE CLEAR by now that I place a heavy emphasis on raising money from individuals. Still, you may be wondering, "What about grants? What about corporate donors?"

The fact is, most of the time raising money from institutions still revolves around your relationship with people. In addition, the core concepts we have discussed in this book (Cultivation, The Ask, Making The Case, Thank You) still directly transfer to presenting yourself and your Ask in an institutional setting.

Let's start with the concept that institutional fundraising still revolves around people. Nearly every institutional giving situation has a person or a group of people who make their funding decisions. These people are the ones who suggest granting priorities and in some cases evaluate applications for funding, and they most certainly are the ones who guide applicants through the process.

Here are some things you need to know.

BASICS

It's imperative that you thoroughly review an organization's giving priorities before you decide to apply. Make sure your work is a fit for their goals. If it's not, do not waste your time or theirs. If it is, by all means, apply.

Second, many artists and art organizations don't approach institutions for grants and gifts because they don't have tax-deductible status. In fact, people can always donate to you whether or not you have been declared a 501(c) 3 charitable organization. If you don't have it, the person simply does not get a tax deduction for your gift. They may very well want to support you and that may or may not be a barrier for those giving. Many granting organizations do not have this flexibility, though. When you are looking into their funding goals, it's important that you look for their funding requirements, as well. If they require a 501(c)3 status to fund you, they will state that very clearly.

It's important to note, however, that not everyone needs to start a charitable organization to qualify for grants and gifts from corporate and organizational sponsors. Take the time to search for a fiscal sponsor, someone who has a 501(c)3 organization and who will be willing to let their organization serve as a pass through for the independent artist and a funder. These fiscal sponsors typically take a small percentage of any income as a fee for the service. Finding a fiscal sponsor may allow you to apply for grants without creating a larger institution around you. This concept is only just now growing in popularity, so it will be important to find out for sure if the organization you are applying to will actually accept this means of donating to you as a viable strategy.

Once you have determined you are a good fit for the organizational priorities, spend some time getting to know the organization and who is involved. Check out their website, Google the company/foundation, and identify the key players in the granting process. Find the program manager, the President or CEO of the organization, or who is on the board. If possible, get to know their priorities and likes.

Knowing who is involved with an organization is important. These are the people who will clarify organizational goals, help you understand what you need to do to apply, and perhaps even make recommendations for funding.

Now, get to know these people. Reach out to the program officer and see if you can set a meeting to discuss your efforts and their organizations. Add these people to your mailing lists and invite them to shows. Keep them up to date with your activities. The more they know about you and your work, the more welcome your application will be. Keep in mind that many funders have small staffs and may not be as available for conversations as those with larger teams.

COMPLETING THE APPLICATION

At some point, based on their instructions, you will have to put together an application for funding. Every organization has its own process, though some are starting to come together and design shared applications. Through your research and conversations, get to know exactly what is required to apply. Then follow those rules *to the letter.* You don't want to have your application rejected because you didn't follow their guidelines.

Most applications include a series of questions that allow you to share your narrative. It's important that you read those questions over very carefully and answer exactly what they are asking for. Make your answers specific and to the point.

For example, if a question asks you to describe your achievements for the last year, do not spend any time talking about what you are planning to do in the next year, even if you think those plans are more exciting than what you've already accomplished. (They're looking for your track record, not your hoped-for goals.) Or if they ask you how you intend to market your production, don't discuss your creative efforts. (If you don't have a marketing plan, take the time to create one. Get help if necessary. They want to know that your efforts—and their donated money—will not go to waste.)

Don't repeat yourself in a proposal just to drive home a point. The decision makers read the full application often many times, and there's no need for you to waste precious space on repetition.

Most grant questions have a specific purpose. Don't venture away from the premise of the question. It will keep your whole application clear and allow the reader to learn what they need to from your writing.

Using their application, try to "Make the Case" for the project you are applying to support. This is no different from making the case for an individual. Reread that chapter of this book before filling out your application, and make sure you keep your messaging concise and focused.

Along those lines, it's also important to make sure you do not exaggerate (or fabricate) information in these applications. There will be a time when a grant application asks you to describe something that you are not doing. (What's the purpose of this? Please explain.) It's best to be honest about your activities and explain why you are not doing a certain kind of project or activity they're inquiring about instead of fabricating an answer you think the application reader wants to hear.

I cannot emphasize this enough, as well: Claiming that you're planning to use an exhibition or performance or a produced piece like a play or CD or DVD as an educational experience or tool when you really have no intention of doing so or have no means of making this happen is, in fact, fraudulent. Sure, you're making it "sound good" to the donor. But it's a bad idea. Just don't do it.

Remember: Most granting organizations require a reporting of activities after the fact, and you don't want to get caught not doing what you said you would do.

It's important for you to stay true to your goals regardless of funding. By doing so, you set yourself up for the greatest long-term success.

GET EARLY FEEDBACK

When you have completed your application, it is always a good idea to take the questions you were asked and the answers you wrote and give both to an unaffected party for feedback. Ask a spouse, a friend, or a colleague in the field. Allow the other person to read through it and provide feedback to your responses. Having another person respond to your writing will often turn up questions or concerns you wouldn't have been able to see because you are so close to it. Listen to the input, and make the changes that you need to make.

When you have completed the application, it's imperative that you submit it by the deadline and according to the organization's instructions. Don't be one day late. That will automatically *disqualify* you. Most grants are highly competitive, and there is no reason to give an organization an excuse to dismiss yours.

WHAT IF. . .?

Two things will happen after you submit your application. Your request will either be accepted or it will be rejected. It's important that you prepare for either possibility. What happens if they say no? How will you fund your project? What if they say yes? Are you ready to implement the plan you proposed?

Whether you get the grant or not, it's still important you say thank you as soon as possible after you receive the notification.

Yes. You still need to thank an organization if you were turned down. The group put in many hours reviewing all the submissions and probably took time out of their busy lives to participate in the decision-making process. That kind of effort is deserving of thanks. It also gives you an opportunity to ask for feedback on your application by asking why it was turned down, so that you can learn how to improve it for the future.

If you received a grant, it's also important to focus on the Thank You. All too often I have seen people apply and receive grants and never thank the organization for the support. Maybe it has something to do with it being an organization and not a person. The fact is, there are still people deeply involved in the process, and those people thought highly enough of you to award you money. I don't know of much that's more worthy of your appreciation.

Make a call to the program director and tell them how much you appreciate their support. Write a letter to the board of directors. Make sure to let them know you will list their organization on all the materials surrounding the project they supported, and follow through on that promise. Invite them to the performance or opening. Thank them early and thank them often. Just like with individual donors, it's the Thank You that will be remembered the next time you apply.

A friend of mine who is a program officer at a major foundation that grants more than $6 million annually to arts organizations recently reinforced the importance of saying "thank you" to me. He recalled working very hard to "fight" for a new organization that was just getting started in his city and wasn't as well known to the foundation's board as other applicants. The organization received the funding, but the program officer didn't hear a thing from the group until they needed money again. How do you think this would make him feel? Do you think he will work as hard the next time?

STAY IN CONTACT

As is true with individuals, it's just as important that you communicate with the organization when you are not asking for money, especially if they have funded you. Keep them up to date with the progress of your project. Let them know how their money is being put to use. Keep them up to date with all your efforts. They want to know what you are doing, and they will want to share that information. Make it easier for them to celebrate the people they support to their key stakeholders. The more they know and understand your efforts, the more likely they are to use you as a justification for their funding. Sometimes simply including the program officers on your organization's newsletter is enough for them to stay up to date on your work.

Please also remember that the people at the giving institution are just that, people. Treat them with the respect you would treat any individual donor. For example, don't corner them at an event and ask why you didn't get funding.

I'm a big believer in fundraising from individuals, but support from grants can be a powerful source of funds that allow you to achieve your goals. Please keep in mind that no grant is guaranteed in perpetuity and there is nothing to say that the grant will be there for you in the next round. Always be conscious of what you will do if the funding goes away one year. I have seen many organizations become fully dependent on grant funding to provide their services. I have also seen some of these organizations suddenly forced to make dramatic organizational decisions when a grant they have received for years didn't materialize.

So, apply to grants when they are a good fit for your effort, but don't limit your fundraising to seeking them. Always look for ways to diversify your giving.

As I've alluded several times, I believe individuals are the key to healthy fundraising. They are diverse and plentiful. They have fewer giving restrictions, and if treated properly are less likely to just go away. Having said that, pursue all opportunities that present themselves for funding.

9

RECRUITING OTHERS

THIS BOOK IS MEANT to empower you to take the leap and start fundraising for your idea or project. By now you have learned to overcome some of the barriers many of us put up to avoid fundraising; gotten to know who your donor is; learned the importance of the Thank You; and understood important it is to keep in touch with your supporters when you're not asking for money. At this point, I am hoping that you feel empowered and inspired to go out there and ASK.

The final thing we need to cover is how to recruit others to fundraise for you. You will eventually come to a place where the goal or the campaign can't be accomplished by you alone. You will need to get others engaged in fundraising for you. This will expand your reach and allow you access to a greater pool of potential supporters.

These supporters might be family members, spouses, volunteers, members of your board, staff members—really anyone who believes in what you are trying to accomplish.

Before you engage anyone to fundraise for you, it's important that you feel confident in your own abilities. To teach someone else, you need to know your subject matter. You will always be your best fundraiser, so I recommend that you embrace the skills laid out in this book before passing the baton on to anyone else.

Talk through all of the concepts I present here with your potential supporters. If you believe in what I am writing, then make sure they believe in it, too, because they will be going down the same path you went down. Make sure they understand the importance of the Thank You, that they tackle their own barriers to asking for money, and most importantly that they understand the giving case you are making.

MAKING THE CASE

Why don't we start with Making the Case, because that's really going to be the place you will need to start with your new recruit. Convince them that your campaign is worthwhile. Make them a believer. While they will never believe to the level you do, they need to get as close as they can and be able to convey their own level of passion for your project.

So spend as much time as is necessary on the case statement. Allow them to pick your brain, ask questions, and even in some cases challenge your assertions. Let them go through their process of assimilating your passion and your ideas. In the end, they will create their own version of your case statement:

a carbon copy of the original, ever so slightly different yet still conveying the same core message. It will become their case statement and something they believe in and sell to their world.

CULTIVATION

When you recruit other people to fundraise, they will be reaching out to one of two groups of people: Those you already have a relationship with and those with whom they themselves are more directly connected.

If you are recruiting someone to fundraise from people who primarily have a relationship with you, you will need to spend some extra time with your recruits to make sure they understand the history of the relationship. Catch them up on conversations, meetings, past giving, and any other relevant history. Make sure you are available to them if they need you, and be ready to jump back into the conversation when it's appropriate. In the end, it's your relationship and one you will want to maintain. Make sure you take time to be a part of the process.

Recruiting someone to fundraise from his or her contacts is a preferable and powerful path. It expands your reach and gives you access to a new world of supporters. It's also very dependent on the person you recruit and their relationship with the prospect. Allow them to set the pace of conversation. Don't pressure them to reach out when it doesn't feel right to them. Encourage them, support them, and let them feel empowered in the process.

THE ASK

Eventually, the people fundraising for you will have to ask for the money. Remember how you felt making your first Ask. Reflect on the fears and barriers that you had to overcome when you first took that leap. Your recruit is feeling the same way, and in some instances may feel it in a more intense way. This isn't their project. Clearly they believe in it and believe in you, but in the end they will never share the exact same conviction that you do.

I believe it's smart, especially in the beginning, for you to join your recruit on the Ask. Your presence will provide a level of comfort for them and for the potential donor. It will also show your dedication to the process. Before you go for an Ask, meet with your fundraiser and talk through the meeting. What will their role be? What will your role be? Make sure you are both on the same page about what you will be asking for.

Then just go for it.

It takes time, but if you are diligent in these early Asks, you will see the recruit coming into his or her own and needing you less and less. It's smart to put the time and effort in early so that long term you have someone who can take some of the fundraising weight off your shoulders. You will never (and honestly should never) push off all fundraising duties. This is your work and your passion. Leveraging the passions and talents of others, however, is always wise.

THANK YOU

The rule of thumb is that whoever made The Ask should

be the first to say "thank you." They were the one who convinced the donor to support, so they should be the first to reach out with their appreciation. This does not absolve you from the task of saying "thank you" as well, though. They are still giving to you and your project, so be sure to reach out yourself and express your gratitude.

As always, you both should strive to make the Thank You as personal and as meaningful as possible. Thank early and thank often.

BUILDING A TEAM

This process starts with you. You are the one with the dreams and visions and in the end, you are the one who will see them through. So take all the time you need to practice the skills in the book and develop a process that you are comfortable with. Get to know yourself, your barriers, and your limitations. It is through your understanding of yourself that you can openly and honestly determine when you need help and how you need help.

As I mentioned earlier in this chapter, at some point you may simply not be able to do it all yourself. That's when you will start thinking about bringing in others (staff, volunteers, board members), to assist you. When you get to this place, keep in mind that fundraising work is not something you should try to pawn off or get someone else to do entirely. If you want sustained fundraising success, you will want to stay a part of the process.

So think through your experiences, and ask yourself:

» Which part of the process was the most difficult for you?

» Did you have a hard time documenting your conversations?

» Were you slow in getting thank-you notes out?

» Did you accomplish very little for fundraising when you were in rehearsal?

» Where did you struggle with the process?

Take this information and use it to shape your support. Let your struggles guide you on an honest assessment of your needs. Be clear about them and define them. That's the help you will need to find—people who will be willing to fill those gaps and make you more effective in your activities.

Depending on where you are in your growth, you can likely get away with finding an intern or a volunteer to provide support. As the activity level grows, you may want to explore hiring someone. Eventually, you might have enough going on that you may need to bring in someone to lead this support system. The main point is that you need to be the guiding force and that the support should be arranged to complement your efforts.

Be careful about falling into a trap of setting up a system larger than what you need right now or one that you see somewhere else. Remember, fundraising is simple, and it does not require massive teams or processes to make it effective. Grow your support organically and build it around your efforts.

It's very important that however you structure your support, there is frequent communication among all of the parties. Make sure everyone is aware what others are doing for the campaign. The last thing you want it to have one person set up a meeting for an Ask while another person is sending the same donor a solicitation letter. Encourage everyone participating to share their activities with everyone else.

YOUR BOARD OF DIRECTORS

My goal in this book is to simplify the fundraising process. I know many of you reading this are independent artists or run very small arts organizations that may never grow to the level necessary to form a 501(c)3 non-profit corporation. Many of you are surely considering moving in this direction, though, or are already structured this way. For a nonprofit, a board of directors is a requirement for obtaining the tax-exempt status and is the body ultimately responsible for the success and failure of an organization. There are hundreds upon hundreds of books about boards and their roles out there. Here I want to touch briefly on some thoughts about a board and its role with fundraising.

A board of directors can be a powerful fundraising arm for any organization. They have made a commitment to steward the organization, volunteering time, money, and energy into its success. They have displayed through their actions a commitment to the organization's goals and visions. What better collection of people to go out there and sell a fundraising campaign?

The key before engaging any board in external fundraising is making 100 percent sure that every member of the board and the organization's staff is on the same page about their roles in any campaign. It's important to discuss and agree on each party's role and responsibilities. Consider:

» Will board members be expected to donate themselves to a campaign?

» Will they also be expected to raise money from their personal networks?

» Are these decisions universal, or will allowances be made for specific members?

Too often I have seen a lack of clarity and transparency trip up great fundraising campaigns. The staff has an expectation that the board is going to take on a lion's share of the work and vice versa—the board believes it's the role of the staff. Work collaboratively in advance of a campaign and make sure the responsibilities are clear. This clarity will allow a campaign to flow smoothly and be successful. You are less likely to have bruised egos, arguments, or frustrations.

In general, it is hugely important to make sure a board of directors as a collective is clear about what their role in fundraising in general will be. If you are forming a new board, work to set the ground rules ahead of time. Already existing collectives should create a document explaining board member fundraising expectations, and all should sign off on it. Then, before bringing in a new member, make sure that person has a clear sense of their fundraising responsibilities *before* they are voted in.

Finally, I recommend that you set a regular process of fundraising coaching with each member. Make sure they understand the importance of all the principles laid out in this book and that they are regularly thinking about prospective donors and cultivating them along for future campaigns.

10

CONCLUSION

IN THE END, fundraising is nothing more than asking for money. It's a simple process, one at which anyone can succeed.

You will find success by enacting any of the tips I wrote about in this book.

> » Learn how to say, "thank you" genuinely and you'll bring donors back more regularly.
> » Ask enough people and you will get the gifts you need.
> » Keep your supporters up to date with your work and you will have a passionate fan base.
> » Convey compelling reasons for giving and you will win over new supporters.

Do all of these things and your success at raising money will grow, as will your confidence in the process. Practice will make it easier, and eventually you will be doing it all without thinking about it.

Now, just take that first step (that leap of faith) and go out there and ask for support.

ACKNOWLEDGEMENTS

This book exists because of some very special people:

Stacey Shifflett

David Hazard, founder of ASCENT, an international coaching and book development program for authors.

Amanda Andere, Michel Bigley, Andrea Burkholder, Naomi Grabel, Inger Hatlen, Zoe Keating, Kate Ahern Loveric, Ricki Marion, Andrew Simonet, Amy Smith, Katie Watkins

All the AccelART artists

DAMIAN SINCLAIR is the President and CEO of AccelART, an innovative fundraising, marketing and business services firm dedicated to advancing the artistic community by accelerating the emergence of culturally relevant individual works.

Damian has dedicated the last 10 years supporting artists and their creative processes. He has worked within a multitude of different managerial roles and artistic fields—consistently driven by his need to support artistic creation.

He is the co-founder of the Capital Fringe Festival and has worked with Pig Iron Theatre Company, The Wilma Theater, Woolly Mammoth Theatre Company, Arena Stage, Greater Reston Arts Center (GRACE) and The Kennedy Center.

Manufactured by Amazon.ca
Bolton, ON

23750508R00057